# WHICH WORD?

## SUSAN QUILLIAM

## James Nisbet

WORDS can be very confusing! Some words sound alike, but are spelt differently, and have various meanings. Some look and sound dissimilar, but are used in ways which are confusing. This book explains the differences between some of these words and helps you learn them and remember which word to use.

The best way to work with this book is not to read it from cover to cover. Instead, concentrate on the words you find most confusing.

**Read** the explanation and examples. Make sure you understand what they are telling you.

**Practise** by doing the exercises.

**Remember** the meanings in *italics* and the memory rhymes.

**Check** your answers, and if they are wrong, read the explanation again. Maybe you need extra help from your teacher.

You will need to know what these words mean in order to use the book.

**Noun**: a naming word.

  If there is only one, the noun is singular; cat, church, woman.

  If there is more than one, it is plural; cats, churches, women.

**Adjective**: a word describing a noun.

  black cat, old church, tall woman.

**Verb**: a doing word.

  It may be present—the cat sleeps; past—the church opened; future—the woman will arrive.

**Adverb**: a word describing a verb.

  sleeps soundly, opened early, will arrive soon.

**Apostrophe**: a punctuation mark. One of its uses is to replace letters missed out when you make one word from two. I am—I'm. She is—She's.

My thanks to the staff of Mabel Fletcher Technical College, especially Gwen Hardman, who provided the original ideas for sections 3, 4, 5, 11, 12, 16, 18 and 22, and to everyone who has given help and support.

# Contents

Published by James Nisbet & Co. Ltd, Digswell Place, Welwyn Garden City, Herts
First Published 1981 © James Nisbet    0 7202 0838 6
Typeset by CCC, printed and bound in Great Britain by William Clowes (Beccles)
Limited, Beccles and London

# Accept Except Expect

**Accept**, beginning with **acc**, means *take what is offered.* If you don't know whether to use accept or not, try replacing it with take. If it fits, accept is the right word to use. You can add endings to make words like acceptable or acceptance.

1. Please accept this gift with my love.
2. The magazine accepted your story? They must be mad!
3. We found the meal quite acceptable, but my Dad threw his spaghetti at the waiter!

**Except**, beginning with **exc**, gives the sense of *apart from.* Replace except with apart from or *but*; if your sentence still sounds right, use except. This word is often followed by words such as 'for' or 'that'. The only other common word with the same beginning is exception—something apart from or unusual.

1. Everyone, except Sam, was happy!
2. The party was good, except that it finished too early.
3. She's always late. Today was an exception—she was on time.

**Expect** is easily confused with except; the **c** and the **p** change places! Expect is a verb meaning *look forward to* or *think it likely that.* Try the replacement test again! There is a word expectation, meaning something you look forward to or think is likely to happen, but you won't need to use it often.

1. He expected lots of presents this Christmas, but no one sent him any.
2. I expect he's worn out after the match.
3. Contrary to everyone's expectations, Mary failed the exam.

> For take, use **a c c** to start,
> **E x c** use for apart,
> But looking forward, then, you see,
> Use expect, with **e x p.**

Complete these sentences with accept, except, or expect.

1. I should like to _____ your offer of a job.
2. I did not _____ to be offered the job.
3. Do you find the idea _____ able, or will you reject it?
4. England _____ s every man to do his duty.
5. They all went out for the evening, _____ Keith.
6. This is the _____ ion that proves the rule.
7. Mr Singh _____ ed my point of view without arguing.
8. I like your jacket, _____ that the colour doesn't suit you.
9. They bought everything they needed, _____ the butter.
10. They _____ ed more people to come to the party.

# Aloud Allowed

With all the words below, you can use the meaning in italics to replace the word you have difficulty spelling, and so find out which one you should use.

**Aloud** is one complete word meaning *out loud*. It's usually used about someone's voice, to show that it can be heard clearly.

1. The vicar spoke the prayer aloud.
2. Don't mumble—say it aloud.
3. I hate people who read their news-papers aloud.

Don't mix up aloud with **a loud**, which is two separate words, not one. Loud here is an adjective meaning *noisy*, and goes with a noun, such as 'bang', 'crash' or 'voice', to describe it as noisy.

1. The firework went off with a loud bang!
2. Suddenly, he was startled by a loud crash.
3. He's a bit deaf, so use a loud voice.

**Allowed** means *permitted*. It's made up of allow with —ed on the end; this makes it sound like aloud, though the meaning is different.

1. You are not allowed to talk in a library.
2. Although the goalkeeper argued, the referee allowed the goal.
3. Are we allowed to stay away from work on Monday?

> Out loud is one word, but noisy is two;
> Aloud has one **l**, one **o** and one **u**.
> If something's permitted, it's one word, you see;
> Allowed has two **l**s and one **w e**.

Complete these sentences with aloud, a loud or allowed.

1. The lion roared _____ as the tiger approached.
2. Miss Robinson says we're not _____ to eat sweets.
3. We suddenly heard _____ noise and the roof fell in!
4. What time are we _____ to leave work today?
5. The boxer shouted _____ to his seconds to throw in the towel.
6. The dog gave _____ bark.
7. My mother told me I was not _____ to go to the party.
8. I hate reading _____; my voice sounds silly.
9. Cars are _____ to park at parking meters.
10. The officer called the soldiers' names _____.

# As   Has

**As** can mean *because* or *while*. Simply replace your problem word with because or while, and if it makes sense, use as.

1. As I was late, I had to run for the train.
2. Dad missed his step as he came down.
3. The phone rang as I was cooking the chips.

As can also give the sense of *similar*. It's particularly used in the expression as . . . as when two things are said to be similar to one another.

1. As I thought, Lakshmi's late again.
2. That cat is as stupid as the dog.

**Has** is a verb which gives the idea of *own* or *possess*.

1. Mr Brown has four cars and three houses.
2. The Tax Inspector has a file on Mr Brown!

Has also gives the sense of *suffer from*.

1. She has measles.
2. Our plumber tripped—now he has a broken leg!

Has is also used with another verb about something in the *past*. The verb shows what was done—'visited', 'poured', and has shows that it was done in the past.

1. He has visited his aunt in hospital several times.
2. It has poured with rain all day!

Has with **to** means *must.*

1. She has to improve, or she'll be in trouble.
2. Roger has to consider other people, not just himself.

Has is used as a *singular* word, with a word meaning one thing or person, or with the words he, she or it.

**Have** means exactly the same as has, but goes with I, you or *plural* words.

1. Those boys who have bicycles must leave them in the playground. (*own*)
2. I have a really bad cold. (*suffer from*)
3. You have put the milk bottles out, haven't you? (*past*)
4. Those chairs have to be returned to the shop. (*must*)

---

For similar, because or while,
Use as—and make it fast.
But has is used for own or must,
For suffer and the past.

---

Complete these sentences with as or has.

1. The child was upset _____ the teacher scolded him.
2. _____ I suspected, he hasn't done any work.
3. He _____ a headache and a backache.
4. She did her homework _____ she was eating her tea.
5. She _____ been to the new supermarket and likes it.
6. Fred _____ to wash the dishes before he can go out.
7. Her eyes are _____ blue _____ the sea.
8. Julie _____ beautiful eyes.
9. _____ she arrived early, she went to the cafe to wait.
10. _____ she said anything about our argument last night?

9

# Hear Here

**Hear** is used to explain what you do with your *ears*. If you put an **h** on the beginning of the word ear, you have the right spelling. The nearest word to it is *listen*.

1. His ears are so big, he hears everything.
2. I hear music every time she walks into the room.
3. My Grandma can hear very well when she wants to.

**Here** gives the idea of in this *place*.
(There and where, which are also about place, are spelt in the same way, so if you remember here, you'll get the other two right as well!)

1. Sit here in this circle.
2. Those books are kept here on the shelf.
3. Here is the file you wanted.

Here is also used in expressions like *here comes* or *here you are.*

1. Here comes Martin—he's been on holiday this week.
2. Here you are—have another cream cake.
3. Here and there around the room, she had placed vases of flowers.

> Listen, an ear
> With an **h** on, you see,
> But here in this place
> Is spelt **h e r e.**

Complete these sentences with hear or here.

1. Philip has been _____ plenty of times.
2. _____comes that man with the brown hat.
3. He can _____ everything we say.
4. I always _____ strange noises late at night.
5. We asked them to meet us _____.
6. My Grandpa is very hard of _____ing.
7. _____ you are; _____ is the book you wanted.
8. We _____ that she's bought a new coat.
9. She's looked _____, there and everywhere for that book.
10. I wish I could _____ what Julie is saying.

# It's Its

**It's** is a shortened form of *it is* or *it has*.

When we speak, we often leave out the **i** or the **ha** and say it's, instead.

When we write that down, we put an apostrophe between the **t** and the **s** to show where the letters are missing. If you can use it is or it has in your sentence, and it makes sense, use it's with an apostrophe.

1. It's nearly time to go home, thank goodness. (it is)
2. It's been a really good day today. (it has)
3. I think it's a shame that it's rained during Wakes Week. (it is, it has)
4. Taiwo says it's a pity you're not well. (it is)

12

**Its**, with no apostrophe, means *belonging to it*. If belonging to it fits in your sentence, use its with no apostrophe. It's the same sort of word as our, their, whose, your.

1. This book has lost its cover.
2. The kitten was chasing its tail, and very nearly caught it!
3. Our football team played its best match last week.

> When it's means it is or it has, there's the trap;
> You need an apostrophe filling the gap!
> But when its means simply belonging to it,
> An added apostrophe just doesn't fit!

Complete these sentences using it's or its.

1. _____ an exciting book.
2. The team lost _____ last six wickets for only twenty runs.
3. _____ stupid to sit talking and never do anything.
4. _____ quite possible for Brian to sleep all day.
5. The dog was howling _____ head off.
6. I think _____ a lovely thing to have happened.
7. The bird was sitting in _____ cage.
8. Their car had _____ brakes tested.
9. He tells me _____ going to be a good party.
10. The school had _____ open day last week.

13

# Later Latter Last

**Later** tells you about the *time* something was done, and is often used with the word 'on'. It has only one **t** in the middle.

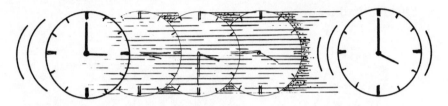

1. You're later than usual for this lesson.
2. I'll talk to you about this later.
3. Later on, we went to Bill's house and played records.

**Latter** means the *second*. When two things are mentioned, the second one is the latter. (The first one is called the former.) Latter is spelt with two **t**s.

1. Kim and Ahmed both came home; the latter watched television.
2. I like apples and oranges, but I prefer the latter.
3. The latter half of the concert was very boring.

**Last** means *final* in a series.

1. The last lesson on Friday is Maths.
2. Philip was the last person to arrive.

Last also means the *most recent* event in the past.

1. The last lesson was boring—this one is interesting.
2. The last party I went to was given by John and Jane.

> Later, (one **t**), talks of time, but then please,
> When you mean second, use latter, two **t**s,
> But for the most recent event in the past,
> Or to say final, you're right to use last.

Complete these sentences with later, latter or last.

1. I'll talk to you _____ about that.
2. Paul and Sally arrived, the _____ wearing black.
3. The _____ time I went to the hairdresser's was a month ago.
4. It's ten o'clock, _____ than I thought.
5. Oranges and lemons are fruit, the _____ being yellow.
6. The _____ coat she bought was expensive, but she'll buy another.
7. The _____ year of the Second World War was 1945.
8. Mrs Brown arrived early; Mr Brown arrived _____ than his wife.
9. The _____ rose of summer often blooms in December.
10. _____ in the evening, he realised his mistake.

# Led Lead

There are two ways of spelling the sound 'led'.

The word **led** means went *in front of, acted as a leader, pulled along*.

1. I led, she followed.
2. He led the demonstration outside the Town Hall.
3. The trainer led the animal very carefully.

**Lead**, spelt with **e a** in the middle, means a type of *metal*. Only use this spelling when you're talking about metal; otherwise, use led.

1. Pass me a lead pencil.
2. The chimney was protected by sheets of lead.
3. Your suitcase is as heavy as lead.

To make it even more confusing, there is another pronunciation for **lead**, which is 'leed'. The rule for this is that you always use the spelling lead for the sound 'leed'—it's only the sound 'led' which has two spellings.

1. Will you lead the way to the manager's office?
2. That dog always fetches his lead when he wants to go for a walk.

P.S. The town name Leeds is an exception to all these rules!

> **Led** correctly gives you 'led'.
> For metal only, use ea instead,
> But for any meaning you may need,
> Always use **lead** for 'leed'.

Complete these sentences with led or lead.

1. Jill _____ the Youth Club Rally last year.
2. _____ paint can be poisonous.
3. Put that dog on a _____ before you go.
4. Yesterday, the girls _____ the way, and we all got lost!
5. Today, we'll let the boys _____.
6. This box is as heavy as _____.
7. Mr Jones _____ the meeting which was held last Tuesday.
8. I want to _____ the march and carry the banner.
9. The vicar always _____s the singing on Sunday.
10. _____ is a dark, weighty metal.

17

# Lie Lay

**Lie**—this word gives the idea of deceit or untruth.
Lie is used as a noun to mean an *untruth*.

1. I cannot tell a lie—I did it with my little hatchet!
2. One lie always leads to another.

Lie is also used as a verb in the present or future, and means *tell an untruth*.

1. To lie about such things is shameful.
2. She will lie her head off to save her skin.

The past of lie, meaning *told an untruth*, is **lied**.

1. When she was questioned, she lied her head off to save her skin.

Lie also gives the sense of *rest in a flat position*. It is a verb that the person or thing does, but not to anybody or anything. You can't lie something down. Lie is always used to talk about present or future time.

1. I lie in bed every morning until ten o'clock.
2. He will lie on the couch all day if you let him.
3. She'd like to lie down, as she feels ill.

To use lie in the past, meaning *rested in a flat position*, the correct word is **lay**.

1. I lay in bed last night.
2. He lay down on the couch all day, because she allowed him to.
3. She lay down, as she felt ill.

**Lay** is also a separate word meaning to *place* or *put*. It's used when the action that a person or thing does is to somebody or something else; in other words, it always has an object. It always refers to present or future time. (Don't confuse it with lay, the past of lie, which means rested in a flat position.)

1. Lay the baby in its cradle.
2. Lay that gun down over there and put your hands up.
3. They will lay the magazines out whichever way you wish.

Don't forget that you use lay in expressions like

Lay the table
Lay an egg.

The past of lay, meaning *placed* or *put*, is **laid**.

1. They laid out the magazines only yesterday.

19

**Remember**;

| Verb | Present, Future | Past |
|---|---|---|
| Lie | Lie<br>An untruth.<br>Tell an untruth. | Lied<br><br>Told an untruth. |
| Lie<br>Never has an<br>object | Lie<br>Rest in a flat<br>position. | Lay<br>Rested in a flat<br>position. |
| Lay | Lay<br>Place or put. | Laid<br>Placed or put. |

Complete these sentences with lie, lay, lied or laid.

1. Mum would like you to _____ the table.
2. I suspect that Keith told me a _____.
3. Last night, I _____ down to relax.
4. Why _____ to Alex when he knows the truth?
5. You _____ there reading as if there's no work to do.
6. I shall _____ the books down here.
7. He _____ to me, so I don't trust him any more.
8. Julie _____ down and put on some sun-tan lotion.
9. He will _____ down as he has a headache.
10. I _____ the table last night, so you must do it now.

# Lightning Lightening

**Lightning** means the electric *flashes* that happen in a thunderstorm. Remember this word has no **e**.

1. My sister is afraid of lightning.
2. The lightning hit the tree in that field.
3. Do you see the lightning flashing over there?

**Lightening**—with an **e** in the middle—means *making light*, either by brightening or reducing (a weight or load). It's the verb lighten, with -ing added to it.

1. The white paint had the effect of lightening the room.
2. Lightening the lorry's load made it easier to drive.

---

Lightning—thunder. Lightening—make light.
Putting an **e** in the second is right!

---

Complete these sentences with lightning or lightening.

1. The weather forecast says there will be thunder and _____.
2. _____ that colour might make the picture seem brighter.
3. Everyone was depressed, but Jim was _____ the gloom by telling jokes.
4. The _____ came very close to the church steeple.
5. The only way to lift that box is by _____ the load inside it.

# Lose Loose

**Lose,** with only one **o**, means *mislay* or *fail to keep*.

1. That child will lose anything you give him!
2. You'll lose your place in the queue if you wander off!
3. Dad always loses his temper when we're home late.

Lose can also mean to *be defeated* in a battle, game or fight.

1. I knew the Blues were going to lose!
2. They'll lose the game if they're not careful!

**Loose,** with two **os**, gives the sense of *free, not fastened, not tight*. It's usually used as an adjective, with nouns, like 'tiger', 'rope', 'skirt'. Very rarely, it's used as a verb, when it means *unfasten* or *let go*.

22

1. Help—the tiger is loose!
2. This rope is loose—tie it up again.
3. That skirt was far too loose on her.
4. Loose that ship from its moorings.

(The word loosen comes from loose, so loosen is always spelt with a double **o**.)

> You'd lose your head if it was loose;
> One **o**, then two—that's right,
> Meaning you would mislay your skull
> If it wasn't fastened tight.

Complete these sentences with lose or loose.

1. I'm trying to _____ weight.
2. Now that I've lost weight, these jeans are really _____ on me.
3. She'll _____ the match if she keeps on making mistakes.
4. You'll _____ your temper if you don't calm down.
5. This wire is _____ and will be dangerous if you don't fix it.
6. The monkey got _____ and disappeared.
7. I knew she'd _____ that umbrella some day.
8. Can you give me some _____ change?
9. _____ that next point and you'll be defeated.
10. That dress was too tight—this one's too _____.

# No Now Know

**No**, beginning with **n**, is generally used in two ways. Firstly, no means the *opposite of yes*.

1. If he proposes, I shall say no.
2. "No, I won't!" said Martin, angrily.

No also gives the sense of *not any* or *none*, and is used before a noun.

1. "I see no ships." said the pirate chief, sadly.
2. There's no reason why I should change my mind.

**Now** refers to time, and has a **w** added at the end. It means *at this minute* or *immediately*. It can also be used in expressions like now and then, now and again, which mean from time to time.

1. Mr Patel is having his lunch now.
2. When he says "now", he means "NOW!"
3. Now and again, they meet for coffee.

24

**Know** is a verb—it can mean *recognise, be friends with* or *be acquainted with.* Remember that it begins with **k** and ends in **w**.

1. I know that girl over there.
2. Everybody in the street knows Mrs Bloggs.

Know can also mean *understand* or *have knowledge of.*

1. He knows that you're feeling angry.
2. It's important for a driver to know how a car works.

> Use **n** for no if you don't agree.
> Add **w**, now, for immediately.
> For friends or understand, use know,
> Add **k** to the start and off you go!

Complete these sentences using no, now or know.

1. We _____ the manager of the shop quite well.
2. It's too late to change your mind _____.
3. There are _____ potatoes left in the dish.
4. To _____ how to speak French is very useful.
5. _____ and then, Neil calls round for coffee.
6. The Head wants this done _____, not next week.
7. They _____ a great deal of Maths compared to us.
8. They _____ all about your situation.
9. _____ football team can beat the Reds.
10. Do you like me, yes or _____?

25

# Off Of

**Off** means *away* or *away from*.

If you're really stuck, and don't know which word to use, decide whether anything's moving; if it is, use off!

1. Mike took the carrier bag off the shelf and gave it to John.
2. She took off her shoes; her sister took them from her.
3. He was sent off for a foul against the referee.

**Of** gives the idea of *belonging to* or *part of a whole*.

1. The father of the boy asked to see the Headmaster.
2. Of them all, I like Winston best.
3. The windows of the car were shattered, but the rest of it was undamaged.

Of can also mean *made from* or *containing*.

1. The Princess's crown was made of gold, rubies and pearls.
2. Mrs Jones gave me a big bag of fruit.

Lastly, of can *go with adjectives*, like 'afraid', 'ashamed' or 'kind', or *verbs*, like 'think', 'approve' or 'suspect'. The list is too long to mention them all. Here are a few examples.

1. I'm not afraid of him.

2. How very kind of you to remember my birthday.
3. My Dad doesn't approve of my latest boyfriend.
4. The police suspect him of smuggling.

Remember that **have**, never of, is used *after* could, must, ought to, should and would.

1. I could have gone to the theatre after all.
2. Tom must have gone home.
3. You should have seen his face!

> If something moves, it's been sent off;
> The **ff**s you need are two.
> With made, belonging and the rest,
> Then of is right for you.
> Have, not of, goes after could,
> Must and ought to, should and would.

Complete these sentences using off, of or have.

1. Try thinking _____ other people for a change.
2. That dog _____ Jim's is very lively.
3. Take that hat _____; it doesn't suit you at all.
4. He gave me a big box _____ chocolates.
5. It was really very good _____ him to drive you home.
6. The car drove _____ slowly, then speeded up.
7. She should _____ apologised to them, but she didn't.
8. My Dad's just fallen _____ the roof!
9. The only one _____ the group who was late was Jacky.
10. They must _____ arrived late, for we missed them.

# Our Hour Are

**Our** means *belonging to us*. It's used in front of a noun to show that it belongs to us. It's the same kind of word as its, their, whose and your. You can also use the word ours, meaning the one (ones) belonging to us.

1. Our teacher has eyes in the back of his head!
2. I think we should take our wellies—it looks like rain!
3. Your books are there, ours are here.

An **hour** is *sixty minutes*. The expression hours, though, is often used to mean a very long time.

1. I'll meet you in an hour—don't be late!
2. The trains to Leeds go every two hours.
3. Jane took hours trying on her new jacket.

**Are** is a verb which is used when you talk about the *present* time. It is usually *plural*, and goes with words meaning more than one thing or person as well as we, you, they, who or which.

1. We are glad you are coming with us to the match.
2. The teachers are on the war-path again!
3. Are you going for your inter-view tomorrow? Good luck!

Are can also be used in special expres-sions such as *here are, there are, here you are, there you are,* which point out things that are important.

1. Here are the boots I like. There are the ones I can afford!
2. There you are—I told you you'd fall flat on your face!

Complete these sentences with our, hour or are.

1. We _____ all going to the match tonight.
2. The appointment will be in one _____'s time.
3. Why do we always miss _____ bus?
4. I think you _____ very lucky.
5. The next bus is in one _____.
6. We all took _____ coats because it looked like rain.
7. There _____ beautiful flowers in the garden.
8. My brother's friends _____ so annoying!
9. This newspaper is _____s; which one is yours?
10. We've been waiting for _____s; well, ten minutes!

# Quiet Quite

**Quiet**, spelt with **iet**, is to do with lack of noise. It's a noun meaning *silence*, and an adjective meaning *hushed*. You can add -er and -est to make quieter and quietest.

1. She needs peace and quiet to recover. (noun)
2. The librarian asked for complete quiet. (noun)
3. The audience was very quiet as the winner was announced. (adjective)
4. The engine of your car is very quiet—is it running? (adjective)

We also use quiet as a way of saying *not busy*, usually about shops, offices, factories.

1. It's been a quiet day at the office.
2. On Saturday afternoon, the shops are usually crowded, but when there's a football match on, they're very quiet.
3. Things are very quiet at the factory at present.

**Quite**, spelt with **ite**, means two different things.

Firstly, it means *completely*. Try replacing quite with completely; if it fits, you're correct.

1. It's quite all right as far as I'm concerned.
2. She felt quite horrified at what had happened.

Quite can also mean *rather* or *partly*, almost opposite to completely! Confusing, isn't it?

1. It took quite a long time.
2. I quite like the scarf which Abdul bought.

> In **e**very **t**ree there is a bird
> Whose song's so qu**iet** it can't be heard.
> **If t**hat **e**xpression isn't right,
> Well then, the word you need is qu**ite**.

Complete these sentences with quiet or quite.

1. The crowd fell completely _____ when the goal was scored.
2. The shops in town were very _____ during the bus strike.
3. Sometimes, Chris _____ likes walking in the park.
4. To revise, you need peace and _____.
5. Peter was _____ happy about the arrangements.
6. " _____ , please." called the teacher; the class obeyed.
7. I think it's _____ important for you to go.
8. Sometimes, Chris likes a _____ walk in the park.
9. Eithne was _____ overcome with fear.
10. Having completed this exercise, you'll be _____ pleased.

# Raise Rise

**Raise** means *lift* or *make something go upwards*. You can, for example, raise a heavy weight.

1. I raise my hand when I want to ask a question.
2. The girder was raised by a crane.
3. He raised his eyebrows at the question.

Raise is also used with other words.

With words like 'topic', 'matter', 'question', raise means *mention*.

1. Tom wishes to raise the matter of the sponsored walk.
2. The teacher raised the question of Betty's absence.

With words like 'money' or 'funds', raise means *collect*.

1. I helped to raise money for the new Church Hall.
2. We held a fund-raising bazaar last week.

When talking about children, raise means *bring up*.

1. In my young day, children were properly raised.
2. He raised his son to be just like him.

**Rise**, spelt without the **a**, means *go upwards*. We also use the word rise when people *get up* out of bed.

1. The birds rise into the sky.
2. The sun will rise at eight o'clock today.
3. Petrol prices will rise next week.
4. Her Ladyship rises at ten each morning.

Rise is also a noun meaning a *movement upwards*.

1. Sunrise is at eight o'clock.
2. There's been another rise in the cost of living.
3. I got a £5 rise this week.

Complete these sentences with raise or rise.
1. They would like to _____ the matter of extra holidays.
2. The court will _____ as the judge enters.
3. _____ your voices in praise when the hymn is played.
4. The manager offered to _____ Neil's salary.
5. I always _____ early in the summer.
6. The crowd began to _____ to its feet.
7. I want to move to the country and _____ kids!
8. Will Frank be able to _____ the money by next week?
9. I always _____ the flag at the start of the ceremony.
10. I think Rob will _____ to a top position in his firm.

# Their There They're

**Their** means *belonging to them*. It's used with a noun, like 'hats' or 'Dad', to show that the hats belong to the people mentioned, or the Dad belongs to them. It's the same sort of word as its, our, whose and your. Theirs means the one (ones) belonging to them.

1. Yvonne and Miriam have their hats on.
2. Their Dad has a new car.
3. These coats are theirs, not ours.

**There** is about *place*. It has the word 'here' in it, which should remind you that it means in that place.

1. Stand there on the spot marked X.
2. Put that parcel over there.

There is also used in expressions like *there is, there are, there was, there were.*

1. There is something about him I really don't like.
2. There were only two people in the whole theatre.

There is can be shortened to **there's**, and an apostrophe takes the place of the missing **i**. Don't confuse this with theirs, which means the one (ones) belonging to them.

1. There's a lovely house on the corner of the street. (There is)
2. Theirs is a lovely house. (The house belonging to them)

**They're** is the shortened form of *they are*. The apostrophe shows that the letter **a** is missing.

1. They're really happy now.
2. They tell me they're bored at home.
3. They're going to Corfu next week.

> **E i** shows belonging—their hats or their hair.
> **E r** in the middle means place—over there!
> Add apostrophe **s** to mean there is, but then
> Don't confuse it with theirs, spelt with **e i** again.
> They are can be shortened to they're straight away;
> Simply add an apostrophe, miss out the **a**.

Complete these sentences with their, there or they're.

1. _____ feet were sore and blistered.
2. The shoes I want to buy are over _____.
3. Will you put _____ books down next to ours.
4. _____ is something very pleasant about Sandra.
5. _____'s really no need for him to go.
6. I'm proud of them; _____ working very hard.
7. We don't like our seats—we prefer _____s.
8. _____ too stupid for words.
9. We arranged to see them by the canteen over _____.
10. I'd like to know what _____ really thinking.

# Two Too To

**Two** is the number word for 2.

1. There are only two examples in this section, not three.
2. The Bingo caller shouted "Two little ducks, twenty-two!"

**Too**. This word means *also*. If you can replace your problem word with also, it's always too.

1. Pass my coat and my scarf too, please.
2. When we saw him, we waved, and he waved, too.
3. Do you want to come to the dance, too?

Too can also mean *excessively* or *more than enough*. It adds strength to adjectives, like 'cold', 'fast', 'many', 'few', 'much'.

1. It's much too cold in here.
2. You drive too fast.
3. Too many cooks spoil the broth.

**To**, first of all, means *towards*, often involving movement of some sort.

1. Take that book over to Jenny, please.
2. Go back to your desk and sit down, boy!
3. He's never very polite to me.

To is also used to *introduce a verb*, like 'go', 'think', 'explain', 'do'.

1. "I want to go home!" wailed the small child.
2. It's hard to think when you're tired.
3. I wish to explain that you don't have to do it.

> For towards and with a verb,
> Spell it **t** and **o**.
> Add **o** for excessively,
> Or to say also.
> If you mean the figure 2,
> Simply add a **w**.

Complete these sentences with two, too or to.

1. After a busy day, we just want _____ rest.
2. We sat down, and they sat down, _____.
3. He put his hand up _____ his face.
4. It was _____ beautiful a day _____ work.
5. There were only _____ classes _____ attend that day, not three.
6. They want _____ leave this place.
7. If she comes _____, then I'm staying here.
8. She has gone _____ the shops.
9. I've only _____ hands—I can't do everything at once.
10. I know _____ much about you.

# Ware Wear Where We're Were

**Ware** means *things for sale*. You'll find it in words like warehouse, which means a place where things for sale are stored. On its own, ware is rare!

1. Is there a hardware shop near here? I've just burnt the kettle!
2. January sale of kitchen ware, all half price!

**Wear** is used about *things you put on*; clothes, jewellery, makeup, a smile, a frown. You can wear a hairstyle or a beard, too! One way of remembering how to spell wear is that, like hear, it has ear in it, so if you think of the following sentence when you're stuck, you might get it right!

In his *ear*, he *wears* a *hear*ing aid.

1. Motor cyclists must wear helmets.
2. She was wearing a really miserable expression.
3. He wears a long beard.

Wear also gives the idea of *spoil* something by using, or *tire* somebody. It's often found in expressions such as wear and tear, wear down, wear out.

1. I hope these heels don't wear down too soon.
2. Go more slowly or you'll wear yourself out!

**Where** means *at, to* or *in which place*. The word here is in it to remind you that it has to do with place, like there. It's also included in expressions such as everywhere and nowhere.

1. I wonder where I left my glasses?
2. Where do you think you're going?
3. I've looked here, there and every-where for that dog.

**We're** is the shortened form of *we are*. An apostrophe (') is put in place of the **a**.

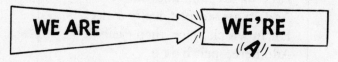

1. We're off to the shops!
2. We're determined that we're going to pass the exam.

**Were** is a verb used when things happen in the *past*, always with words meaning more than one thing or person, and we, you, they, who or which. It has no apostrophe, so don't confuse it with we're, which does have one.

1. The best students were Simon and Mary.
2. The girls were working harder than the boys.
3. They were very cheerful while they waited.

39

Were is also used in the expression *there were*.

1.  There were too many people in the shop.
2.  If there were any dresses left, I'd buy one.

> If this spelling troubles you,
> Start off with a **w**.
> First, add **a r e** as well,
> That gives ware, which you can sell.
> Add an ear instead, and that
> Means you wear a coat or hat.
> Take we are, and miss out **a**,
> Add an apostrophe, we're away!
> For in which place, then easily,
> Add here, spelt **h e r e**.
> When something happens in the past,
> Add **e r e** and that's the last.

Complete these sentences with ware, wear, where, we're or where.

1.  The _____ house was full of food stocks.
2.  Those keys will _____ holes in your pockets.
3.  _____ all dressed up, but we've no _____ to go.
4.  I know that they _____ hoping to go out tonight.
5.  I'll _____ my brown boots with this coat.
6.  Waiter, there _____ three flies in my soup!
7.  _____ did you get that hat?
8.  They _____ at a loss for words.
9.  _____ do you think you're going?
10.  _____ at a loss for something to do, aren't we?

# Weak Week

**Weak.** This is spelt with **ea**, and gives the sense of *without strength.* It can be used about a thing, animal or person, or about an idea or argument. You can add -er or -est to make weaker or weakest.

1. This floor is weak—it'll collapse at any minute!
2. That plan of Bob's is very weak—it simply won't work.
3. He's the weakest person I know; he never keeps his word.

**Week.** This is a period of *seven days.* Remember that seven has two **e**s in it, and so has week.

1. He's taking a week's holiday.
2. They visited us the week before last.
3. Jill says it will take two weeks to do all that work.

Weak **ea** and week **ee** often are confused.
Remember that for seven days, double **e** is used!

Complete these sentences with weak or week.

1. I feel really _____ from lack of food.
2. What you need is a _____'s rest.
3. The _____est link in the chain broke first.
4. He's very _____ at English, but good at Maths.
5. A _____ or two later, he wrote to her again.

# Weather Whether

**Weather**, spelt with **ea**, is the general term for things like *sun, wind, rain* or *snow*.

1. The weather has been really sunny today—we all wore our shorts!
2. During the exams, the weather is always fine.
3. I love the snow and the cold weather.

Weather can also mean *wear down* by the weather, as when stone is worn away by the rain.

1. The wind will weather that boat if you don't protect it.
2. The paint on our house has been weathered by the sun.

Weather can also mean *survive* or *come safely through*, but you will hardly ever need to use it in that way.

1. I hope those yachts weather the storm.

**Whether**, spelt with **he**, *introduces* or *joins* part of a sentence which tells or asks what might happen. It's often followed by 'or' or 'or not'. The simplest way to find out if whether is the word you mean is to replace it by *if*; if the sentence makes sense, you're right!

1. I don't know whether the Reds will win the Cup this year.
2. Whether it's wet or dry doesn't matter.
3. Will you see whether Graham's here or not.

> Weather—**ea**—is the sun and the rain
> And the wind on a boat or a cliff.
> Weather—**ea**—can mean to survive,
> But whether—**he**—means if.

Complete these sentences with weather or whether.

1. _____ he arrives or not, I'm going to the party.
2. The bad _____ made us cancel the picnic.
3. Steve wants to know _____ you still want to borrow his car.
4. The outdoor swimming pool was open in all kinds of _____.
5. The outdoor swimming pool was open _____ or not it was raining.
6. The bad _____ stopped us going on the trip.
7. I insist on knowing _____ or not you like Sandy.
8. On Sunday, the _____ was stormy.
9. _____ they play football well, I really don't know.
10. If the _____ is fine, we shall play football today.

# Who's Whose

**Who's** is the short form of *who is* or *who has*. The apostrophe replaces the missing letters **i** or **ha**, and goes exactly where they were.

1. Who's going to clean up this mess? (who is)
2. Who's been walking all over the floor in muddy boots? (who has)
3. There's the teacher who's put us in detention. (who has)

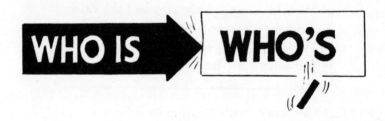

**Whose** is a word which shows *belonging*. When you use it, you mean belonging to a person. It's the same sort of word as its, our, their and your. It's not a short form of any word, so has no apostrophe.

1. There's the teacher whose dog ran away.
2. I wonder whose jacket this is.
3. There's the boy whose friend I went out with yesterday.

Who is and who has
Are too long to be said.
An apostrophe goes
In the middle instead,
But when whose means belonging;
Whose jacket, whose friend,
Simply copy down who
With **s e** on the end.

Complete these sentences with who's or whose.

1. _____ lent Buchi that bike, I wonder?
2. Do you know _____ coming to the party?
3. _____ glass is that?
4. _____ going to tell Fred that we didn't post his coupon?
5. Tell him _____ attended every lesson this term!
6. I saw the milkman _____ van is painted green.
7. He is the man _____ dog bit Des.
8. _____ in charge here?
9. There's the striker _____ playing won them the Cup.
10. Tell me _____ scored the most goals this season.

# Your You're

**Your** means *belonging to you.* It has no apostrophe, and no **e** on the end. It's usually used with a noun, like 'mother' or 'friend'. It's the same sort of word as its, our, their and whose. Yours means the one (ones) belonging to you, and it has no apostrophe either.

1. Your mother wants to see you.
2. Who's your friend?
3. Is this suitcase yours?

**You're** is the shortened form of *you are.* The apostrophe is placed exactly where **a** was.

1. You're happy today—what happened?
2. If you're going to the shops, can you buy some bread?
3. Cheng wants to know if you're willing to see him.

> **Your** means belonging to you,
> Your mother, your friend or your case.
> If you are is too long, then the **a** disappears,
> An apostrophe goes in its place.

Complete these sentences with your or you're.
1. If you do that again, _____ going to regret it.
2. Was it _____ brother who won the three-legged race?
3. Is this pencil mine or _____s?
4. It's _____ turn to buy the ice-creams.
5. I do hope that _____ always happy.

# Answers

p. 5
1. accept
2. expect
3. accept
4. expect
5. except
6. except
7. accept
8. except
9. except
10. expect

p. 7
1. aloud
2. allowed
3. a loud
4. allowed
5. aloud
6. a loud
7. allowed
8. aloud
9. allowed
10. aloud

p. 9
1. as
2. As
3. has
4. as
5. has
6. has
7. as  as
8. has
9. As
10. Has

p. 11
1. here
2. Here
3. hear
4. hear
5. here
6. hear
7. Here here
8. hear
9. here
10. hear

p. 13
1. It's
2. its
3. It's
4. It's
5. its
6. it's
7. its
8. its
9. it's
10. its

p. 15
1. later
2. latter
3. last
4. later
5. latter
6. last
7. last
8. later
9. last
10. Later

p. 17
1. led
2. Lead
3. lead
4. led
5. lead
6. lead
7. led
8. lead
9. lead
10. Lead

p. 20
1. lay
2. lie
3. lay
4. lie
5. lie
6. lay
7. lied

8. lay
9. lie
10. laid

p. 21
1. lightning
2. Lightening
3. lightening
4. lightning
5. lightening

p. 23
1. lose
2. loose
3. lose
4. lose
5. loose
6. loose
7. lose
8. loose
9. Lose
10. loose

p. 25
1. know
2. now
3. no
4. know
5. Now
6. now
7. know

8. know
9. No
10. no

7. quite
8. quiet
9. quite
10. quite

6. to
7. too
8. to
9. two
10. too

10. weather

p. 45
1. Who's
2. who's
3. Whose
4. Who's
5. who's
6. whose
7. whose
8. Who's
9. whose
10. who's

p. 27
1. of
2. of
3. off
4. of
5. of
6. off
7. have
8. off
9. of
10. have

p. 33
1. raise
2. rise
3. Raise
4. raise
5. rise
6. rise
7. raise
8. raise
9. raise
10. rise

p. 40
1. ware
2. wear
3. We're   where
4. were
5. wear
6. were
7. Where
8. were
9. Where
10. We're

p. 46
1. you're
2. your
3. your
4. your
5. you're

p. 29
1. are
2. hour
3. our
4. are
4. hour
6. our
7. are
8. are
9. our
10. hour

p. 35
1. Their
2. there
3. their
4. There
5. There
6. they're
7. their
8. They're
9. there
10. they're

p. 41
1. weak
2. week
3. weak
4. weak
5. week

p. 43
1. Whether
2. weather
3. whether
4. weather
5. whether
6. weather
7. whether
8. weather
9. Whether

p. 31
1. quiet
2. quiet
3. quite
4. quiet
5. quite
6. Quiet

p. 37
1. to
2. too
3. to
4. too   to
5. two   to

48